OFFICIAL

HANDBOOK

FOR

VISITORS

Philadelphia

EDITED BY ROBERT H. WILSON

sponsored by

GIRARD TRUST BANK

and

INDEPENDENCE HALL ASSOCIATION

HAMMOND®
INCORPORATED
MAPLEWOOD, NEW JERSEY   07040

ACKNOWLEDGMENTS

This book includes historical information and photographs assembled for the Independence Hall Association by Harold D. Eberlein and Cortlandt V. D. Hubbard. Additional editorial and illustrative material has been provided by a great many other individuals, institutions, and organizations, and the assistance of all is gratefully acknowledged. The editor's particular thanks are due the following organizations: American Philosophical Society · City of Philadelphia—Office of the City Representative and Director of Commerce · Colonial Philadelphia Historical Society · The Convention and Visitors Bureau of the Chamber of Commerce of Greater Philadelphia · Estate of Stephen Girard · The Free Library of Philadelphia · The Germantown Historical Society · The Historical Society of Pennsylvania · Independence National Historical Park · Library Company of Philadelphia · Chas. P. Mills and Son Photography, Inc. · Pennsylvania Historical and Museum Commission · Philadelphia City Planning Commission · Philadelphia Museum of Art · Philadelphia Yearly Meeting of the Religious Society of Friends.

Third Printing

This book was set in Caslon type, an early typeface used by Benjamin Franklin.

CONTENTS

MAP I
CENTER CITY

SCALE OF MILES

0   ¼   ½

C   **D**

FAIRMOUNT AVE.

Edgar Allan Poe House

GREEN ST.
GARDEN
RIDGE
NOBLE
CALLOWHILL
SPRING
WALLACE

VINE ST.

St. Michael-Zion German Lutheran Church   FRANKLIN SQUARE   St. George's Church

BENJAMIN FRANKLIN BRIDGE To Camden →
30

RACE ST.

Police Administration Bldg.

CHERRY

Site of Old Zion Lutheran Church   Betsy Ross House   Elfreth's Alley

ARCH

Franklin's Grave

Free Quaker Meeting House   Friends Meeting House

FILBERT   Christ Church Burial Ground   Christ Church

INDEPENDENCE NATIONAL

Union Terminal   Reading Terminal

MARKET   HISTORICAL PARK   ST.

Girard Block   Site of Presidential Mansion   Site of Declaration House   Site of Robert Morris House   Wax Museum

Mercantile Library   Atwater Kent Museum   Maritime Museum

Supreme Court Bldg.   Second Bank   U.S. Custom House

CHESTNUT   Congress Hall   New Hall

Jefferson Medical College   Independence Hall   First Bank

Walnut St. Theater   Philosophical Hall   Carpenters' Hall   Site of Tun Tavern

Library Hall

WALNUT   Dolley Madison House   Philadelphia Exchange

Bishop White House

WASHINGTON   Phila. Contributionship   Old St. Joseph's Church

Athenaeum

Tomb of the Unknown Soldier   SQUARE   Powel House

LOCUST   Shippen-Wistar House   SOCIETY HILL

Historical Society   Mikveh Israel Burial Ground   St. Mary's Church

Pennsylvania

SPRUCE

Pennsylvania Hospital

PINE

DELAWARE RIVER

U.S.S. Olympia

Old Pine St. Church   St. Peter's Church   Head House

LOMBARD

SOUTH

BAINBRIDGE

FITZWATER

To Old Swedes' Church

12TH 11TH 10TH 9TH 8TH 7TH 6TH 5TH 4TH 3RD 2ND FRONT DELAWARE AVE.

1   2   3   5

MAP II
GREATER
PHILADELPHIA

SCALE OF MILES

0 2 4 6 8 10

© C. S. HAMMOND & CO., Maplewood, N.J.

7

THE QUAKER CITY OF WILLIAM PENN

The most prominent landmark in Philadelphia is the huge statue of the founder, William Penn, on City Hall Tower. (*Map I-B2*)

Penn was born into a wealthy and influential British family in 1644. Early in life he joined the Religious Society of Friends (Quakers) and turned to religious writing and teaching. He served several terms in prison for his beliefs, and he began to plan a colony in the new world where all men could enjoy religious and political freedom.

In 1681, Penn was granted a province in America in settlement of a debt King Charles II owed his father. The King named the province Pennsylvania or "Penn's Woods."

William Penn was an organizer and statesman as well as religious leader. He planned his city and his province in detail. He signed charters granting self-government and religious freedom. He named his capital city Philadelphia meaning "City of Brotherly Love."

Penn's principles were incorporated later in the Declaration of Independence and the Constitution of the United States. Jefferson called Penn "the greatest lawgiver the world has produced."

City Hall and Penn Statue

The Statue on the Ground in 1893

Pennsylvania was established without war or bloodshed. Penn's belief in human brotherhood guided his dealing with the Indians. His honesty and fairness won their respect.

One of the treasures at the Historical Society of Pennsylvania (*Map I-C3*) is this letter which Penn sent to "the King or Kings of the Indians" before his first visit to America.

My Friends   *London: 18th 8th Mth: 1681*

*There is one great God and Power that hath made the world and all things therein, to whom you and I and all People owe their being and well being, and to whom you and I must one Day give an account, for all that we Doe in the world; this great God hath written his Law in our hearts by which wee are taught and commanded to Love and help and Doe good to one another and not to Doe Harm and Mischief one unto another * * * *

I shall shortly come to you myself at what time wee may more Freely and Largely Confer and Discourse of these matters: in the mean time I shall send my Commissioners to treat with you about Land and afirm a League of Peace: Let me Desire you to be kind to them and the People, and Receive those presents and tokens which I have sent to you as a Testimony of my good will to you and my resolution to live justly, peaceably, and Friendly with you.*

I Am your Loving Friend
Wm Penn

For the King or Kings of the Indians in Pennsylvania

PENN'S WAMPUM BELT

The Indians gave Penn this wampum belt as a token of friendship, the beaded design showing a firm handclasp of red man and white man. It is now in the museum of the Historical Society.

"PENN'S TREATY WITH THE INDIANS"

This painting is known through-out America. The original is in the Pennsylvania Academy of the Fine Arts in Philadelphia. (*Map I-B2*) Although not completely accurate historically, it portrays faithfully the spirit of Penn's government.

The painting is by the Quaker artist, Benjamin West, who was born in 1738 in a house which still stands on the Swarthmore College campus near Philadelphia. (*Map II-B3*) West spent most of his life at the British court and was first president of the Royal Society of London.

The tree in the painting was known as the "Treaty Elm" and stood for more than a century after Penn's time on the riverfront near a street named Shackamaxon. This is one of many Indian names still used in Penn's city. The elm blew down in 1810, but visitors will find the location marked by a stone monument in Penn Treaty Park. (*Map III-C3*)

PENNSBURY MANOR

As proprietor and governor of Pennsylvania, Penn lived at this handsome country estate on the Delaware River above his city. (*Map II-D2*)

During Penn's later years in England, Pennsbury fell into disuse and was torn down. The estate has now been restored and furnished under the leadership of the Pennsylvania Historical and Museum Commission.

OLD MERION MEETING

The oldest house of worship still in use in Pennsylvania is the Merion Quaker Meeting House dating back to 1695. (*Map II-B2*) Tradition says that Penn spoke here. Meetings for worship are held every Sunday or "First-day."

SWEDISH SETTLERS PRECEDED PENN

Nearly fifty years before William Penn founded Philadelphia in 1682, Swedish settlers established the colony of New Sweden on the Delaware River. (Dutch colonists came even before the Swedes, but did not leave a permanent settlement.)

Peter Minuit was the first governor of New Sweden. He led the colonists ashore on March 29, 1638 after purchasing land from the Indians. He built Fort Christina near Wilmington. In 1642, the third governor, Johan Printz, moved the capital of New Sweden to Tinicum Island, now in Pennsylvania. The colony flourished for seventeen years, but the rule of the Swedes came to an end when Peter Stuyvesant led a conquering Dutch expedition up the Delaware in 1655. The Dutch in turn were overthrown by the English in 1664.

Not far from Tinicum, in what is now South Philadelphia, is the handsome headquarters building of the American-Swedish Historical Foundation and Museum. Some reminders of the Swedish settlers may be seen in the Philadelphia area including five of their early churches. See Gloria Dei (pp. 28-29), St. James, Kingsessing (p. 34) and Old Swedes', Wilmington (p. 123).

Typical Settler's Home in New Sweden

American-Swedish Historical Museum (Map III-B4)

Peter Minuit establishes New Sweden, 1638.

William

The historic Liber
Independence Hall, P
bears a Biblical inscripti
claim liberty throughou
land . . ."

Few people realize, howe
the great bell and its me
words originally commemora
liberty that William Penn g
to the settlers of Pennsylvani
bell with its prophetic me
hung in the tower of the Pen
vania State House for twenty
years before American indepe
ence was born.

Penn had granted a charter of
liberties and privileges to his province in 1701. On the fiftieth anni-
versary of that charter in 1751, the
Pennsylvania Assembly ordered a
commemorative bell. A particularly
appropriate Biblical verse, Leviti-
cus 25:10, was chosen. It begins
"And ye shall hallow the fiftieth
year, and proclaim liberty through-

PHILADELPHIA

Penn's Plan of 168

OF PENNSYLVANI

The City PH

out all the land unto all the inhabitants thereof . . ."

This message was already in-
scribed on the bell when it rang out
to proclaim American independence
in 1776.

Penn's charter of liberties is still preserved in Philosophical Hall. (Map I-D2)

IA IN AMERICA, DIVIDED INTO

ADELPHIA *two Miles in Length and one in Breadth*

Schoolkill River

Delaware River

Sᵗ Mathias Vincent

k Benja Furlow

I H E

The Dutch Township

This plan of Philadelphia was made in 1681 by Penn's surveyor, Thomas Holme, whose name is now carried by the section of Philadelphia called Holmesburg. (*Map II-C2*) It is preserved at the Historical Society of Pennsylvania. (*Map I-C3*)

Holme's plan clearly shows Penn's concept of his city as "a greene Country Towne" with straight, treelined streets and well-planned open spaces. There was to be a center square for the "public buildings," and a corresponding open space in the middle of each of the city's quadrants.

Today the city hall stands in the center appropriately named Penn Square. (*Map I-B2*) The other four open spaces still exist in the modern city. In the northwest quadrant is Logan Circle (*Map I-B2*) named for James Logan, one of Pennsylvania's greatest men. (p. 22) In the northeast quadrant is Franklin Square (*Map I-C1*); in the southeast Washington Square (*Map I-C3*); and in the southwest Rittenhouse Square (*Map I-B3*) named for David Rittenhouse, Philadelphia mathematician and scientist.

Rittenhouse Square

Logan Circle

Franklin Square

Washington Square

PHILADELPHIA STILL "THE QUAKER CITY"

Philadelphia Yearly Meeting

For nearly three hundred years Penn's city of Philadelphia has continued to be a center of Quaker thought and activity. Throughout the city and suburbs there are Quaker meeting houses where Meetings for Worship are held weekly and where Meetings for Business are conducted each month.

The first Quaker meeting houses in Philadelphia have long since been replaced. Some of the oldest surviving meeting houses are to be seen in the area surrounding the city, but three colorful places of Quaker worship are still found in the heart of downtown Philadelphia—at 4th and Arch Streets, at 15th and Race Streets, and on 12th Street near Market.

At the Arch Street Meeting House Friends still gather as they have for nearly three hundred years for the Philadelphia Yearly Meeting. A number of exhibits relating to Quaker history may be seen.

Philadelphia is the headquarters of the American Friends Service Committee which directs humanitarian projects of many kinds in the United States and abroad. Quaker-founded schools and colleges are numerous throughout the Philadelphia area.

LEADING CITY OF THE COLONIES

Philadelphia became the largest, wealthiest, and most cultured city in the American colonies, and much of the old Colonial city still remains intact in the midst of the modern metropolis.

Visitors can walk the same streets, see the same public buildings, worship in the same churches, and visit in many of the same houses that stood here long before the American Revolution.

A tour of the historic sections of Philadelphia truly constitutes a trip back to Colonial America.

The Head House of old Second Street Market. (Map I-D3)

King George II still watches over the Colonial city. (Second Street near Market)

A Colonial Parlor—*A handsome house at 217 Spruce Street, built in 1758, is the home of Mr. and Mrs. C. Jared Ingersoll. Mr. Ingersoll's great-great-grandfather was a signer of the Constitution.*

THE POWEL HOUSE

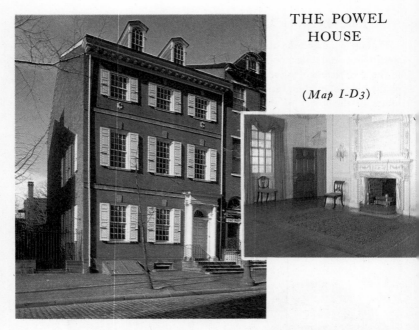

(Map I-D3)

One of the most fashionable houses of Colonial Philadelphia still stands at 244 South Third Street. It was built in 1765 and was the home of Samuel Powel, a wealthy property owner who was mayor of the city in 1776.

Samuel Powel continued to occupy a rear wing of the house during 1777 and 1778 when the mansion was taken over by the British Lord High Commissioner. After the Revolution, Powel was again elected mayor—the first to hold that office under the new government.

The Powels became personal friends of George and Martha Washington. The Washingtons were often entertained in this house, and the Powels in turn visited at Mount Vernon. Washington on occasion occupied the Powel family pew at nearby St. Peter's Church.

In the garden of the Powel House is a pear tree which is as old as the house itself.

ELFRETH'S ALLEY   (*Map I-D2*)

After William Penn divided his city into large square blocks, many property owners added narrow alleys and "courts" between the streets.

This little alley, only one block in length, was cut through around 1700 and has remained virtually unchanged, its houses continuously used since Colonial days. Homes built for Colonial workingmen still serve as private residences today.

There are no mansions in this street. These were homes of river pilots, blacksmiths, tailors, cabinet-makers and pewterers. One house has an open-air gallery above the front door, where the women did their spinning.

21

STENTON—HOME OF JAMES LOGAN (*Map III-B2*)

One of the most influential men in early Pennsylvania was James Logan. As a young man he was secretary to William Penn. In his old age he was friend and adviser to Benjamin Franklin.

For fifty years Logan was agent and representative of the Penn family in America. He held many offices, including president of the provincial council and Chief Justice of Pennsylvania. He was also a successful businessman, making a fortune in fur trading and the iron business.

After he married at the age of forty, Logan bought a tract of five hundred acres of forest land north of Philadelphia and there built

Stenton, one of the finest of Philadelphia's surviving Colonial mansions. Stenton is now owned by the city of Philadelphia. It is beautifully furnished and maintained by the Society of Colonial Dames of America in the Commonwealth of Pennsylvania.

James Logan was a brilliant scientist and scholar. He knew Greek and Hebrew as well as French and Spanish. He corresponded in Latin with learned men abroad. He collected at Stenton the finest library in the American colonies, and left it at his death to the people of Philadelphia. Called the Loganian Library, it is still intact at the main building of the Library Company of Philadelphia. (p. 46)

OLD GERMANTOWN
(Map ·III-B2)

William Penn in 1683 deeded a tract of land northwest of Philadelphia to thirteen families of German settlers led by Francis Daniel Pastorius. They established the community of Germantown which had a long, independent history before being consolidated into the city. Germantown was one of our earliest industrial centers.

The Original Settlers—*Statues on the monument in Vernon Park to Pastorius and the thirteen original families of Germantown.*

Rittenhouse Cottage—*Built in 1707 by William Rittenhouse who operated nearby the first paper mill in America. His great-grandson, David Rittenhouse, mathematician and scientist, was born here in 1732.*

Mennonite Meeting House—*Some of the original settlers of Germantown were German Quakers, or Mennonites. They established the first Mennonite Meeting in America in 1683. This building dates back to 1770.*

Germantown Academy—*This original building, built in 1760, is still used for classes. (Map III-B2)*

Market Square, Germantown—*Laid out in 1703. Here were the market sheds, the firehouse, jail, and stocks of old Germantown. In background at left is the first brick residence in Germantown, now the headquarters of the Germantown Fire Insurance Company.*

Upper Burying Ground—*Some of Germantown's first settlers are buried here. In the background is Concord schoolhouse built in 1775.*

Grumblethorpe—*In 1744, John Wister, a prosperous Philadelphia merchant, built this fine house in Germantown as a summer residence—the first of many there. Stone was quarried on the property, and woodwork came from the trees of "Wister's Woods," which are still to be seen.*

SOCIETY HILL

William Penn chartered a land promotion company called the Free Society of Traders to develop a section of Philadelphia on a slight rise of ground overlooking the Delaware. This became known as Society Hill. Today it is the scene of one of America's most remarkable urban redevelopment projects. In an area covering many city blocks, almost all buildings except those of Colonial origin are being torn down. Those remaining are being restored to their original appearance so that, within walking distance of Independence Hall, visitors may see the old city as it was before the Revolution.

25

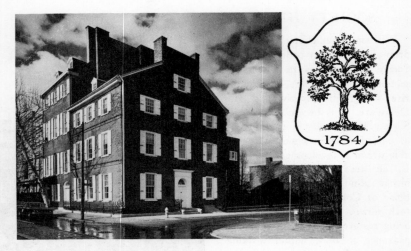

HISTORIC SHIPPEN-WISTAR HOUSE   (*Map I-D3*)

Among the most historic residences in old Society Hill is this home built about 1750. At the time of the Revolution it was occupied by Dr. William Shippen, one of the Pennsylvania delegates to the Continental Congress which met just a few blocks from his home.

Dr. Shippen's son, also a physician, was director general of hospitals for the Continental army. The wife of the younger Dr. Shippen was Alice Lee of Stratford Hall, Virginia. When two of her brothers came to the Continental Congress as delegates from Virginia they stayed in this house and it became the center of the cause of Independence.

Twenty years later, this same house became the home of another great Philadelphia physician, Dr. Caspar Wistar, who was a president of the American Philosophical Association. The wistaria vine is named for him. A scholar and a genial host, he began the evening gatherings called "Wistar Parties" which are still held in Philadelphia.

This house is now occupied by the Mutual Assurance Company for Insuring Houses from Loss by Fire. It was founded in 1784 and its emblem or fire mark is the "Green Tree" which is seen on many Philadelphia buildings.

JOHN BARTRAM'S GARDEN   (*Map III-B3*)

This is the home of another famous Philadelphian of the Colonial era, John Bartram, the botanist. A farm boy, largely self-taught, he became the correspondent and friend of prominent people in Europe and America. He traveled throughout the colonies, collecting trees and plants for his small plantation along the Schuylkill.

In the midst of Bartram's garden there still stands the sturdy stone house originally built by Swedish settlers. Bartram added to it in 1729 and again in 1770. He carved in a stone beneath one of its windows a statement of his faith: "It is God alone, Almyty Lord The Holy One by Me Ador'd."

THE COLONIAL CHURCHES

Old Swedes' Church, *Delaware Avenue near Christian Street*

GLORIA DEI (OLD SWEDES') CHURCH (*Map III-C3*)

The oldest surviving Colonial church within city limits of modern Philadelphia is Gloria Dei or Old Swedes' Church, a memento of the early Swedish settlements along the Delaware. On this site in 1677 the Swedes built a log church whose walls were provided with loopholes for defense.

In 1698 the present church was begun on the same site. It was dedicated in 1700 and later English settlers called it "a cathedral in the forest." Today it is an island of quiet and charm in the busy port area of modern Philadelphia.

The church's original font is located close to the altar. The vestry contains rare Bibles and historic relics. On the front of the organ gallery are two historic items brought from Sweden by early settlers—a carving of two wide-eyed cherubs and an opened Bible with Christmas quotations in Swedish.

Old Swedes' Church has been declared a national historic site. It serves an active Episcopal parish with services every Sunday.

OLD ST. JOSEPH'S CHURCH
(*Map I-D3*)

St. Joseph's, first Roman Catholic Church in Philadelphia, was founded in 1733 at a time when Catholic worship was forbidden everywhere else in America and Great Britain. The Council of Pennsylvania, relying on Penn's Charter of Privileges, refused to close the church as demanded by the governor. Thus they sustained the principle of religious freedom in Philadelphia. The church has been rebuilt twice, but its old-fashioned gateway entrance at 321 Willing's Alley, near 4th and Walnut Streets, preserves the feeling of the church of Colonial days.

St. Mary's Church (*Map I-D3*)

Thirty years after St. Joseph's was established, a second Catholic Church, St. Mary's was built a block away. This church, too, has since been rebuilt, but the old graveyard surrounding it remains unchanged. Commodore John Barry (p. 60) is buried here.

St. Peter's Church—*In this church at 3rd and Pine Streets, completed in 1761, visitors may still see the original high box pews including Number 41 which George Washington sometimes occupied as guest of Samuel Powel. (p. 20) The spire of St. Peter's dominates the Society Hill residential area. In the churchyard are the graves of Stephen Decatur, naval hero, and John Nixon, who proclaimed the Declaration of Independence. (p. 63; Map I-D3)*

Mikveh Israel Burial Ground—*On land originally granted by the Penn family is the old burial ground of Congregation of Mikveh Israel, first Jewish religious community in Philadelphia. Mikveh Israel is presently located in its synagogue at Broad and York Streets.*

This old cemetery, still appearing as it did in Colonial-times, contains the graves of many early Philadelphians of Jewish faith including the patriot, Haym Salomon. (Map I-C3)

31

CHRIST CHURCH   *Second Street, North of Market (Map I-D2)*

Silver Pieces Presented by Queen Anne

1744 Chandelier

Christ Church Bells

Franklin was one of the managers. Its bells were pealed to proclaim the adoption of the Declaration of Independence.

Franklin's family had a pew in Christ Church, as did Washington. Seven signers of the Declaration of Independence are buried in the burial grounds: Franklin, Joseph Hewes, Francis Hopkinson, Robert Morris, George Ross, Benjamin Rush, and James Wilson.

Christ Church owns many historic items including a collection of religious books brought from England in 1696 constituting the first lending library in Pennsylvania.

Christ Church was organized in 1695 and is generally regarded as the most historic of Philadelphia's Colonial churches. The present building, begun in 1727, is an outstanding example of the best in Colonial architecture.

The church tower and spire were added in 1754, financed by a lottery of which Benjamin

Trinity Church—1711
Oxford
(*Northeast Philadelphia*)
(*Map III-C1*)

Old Pine Street Church
—1768
(*Map I-D3*)

St. James Church—1760
Kingsessing (*West Philadelphia*) (*Map II-A4*)

Old St. David's—*1715*
Radnor (*Map II-B2*)

St. George's Church—1769
(*Map I-D1*)

34

THE COUNTRY MANSIONS

LEMON HILL   (*Map IV-C4*)

Among Philadelphia's historic treasures are numerous country mansions and estates preserved intact from Colonial days. Half-a-dozen of these, authentically furnished, are located in Fairmount Park, and are open to visitors on tours arranged through the Philadelphia Museum of Art.

One of the best known is Lemon Hill. This was once the estate of Robert Morris, a friend of Washington and financier of the Revolution. Morris lived here nearly thirty years and raised in his greenhouse the lemon trees which gave the place its present name.

Oval Parlor at Lemon Hill

Like several other old mansions in Fairmount Park, Lemon Hill is situated within ten minutes of downtown, modern Philadelphia.

WOODFORD MANSION *(Map IV-C3)*

This was the home of William Coleman, merchant, lawyer, judge, and friend of Benjamin Franklin. Franklin said of Coleman that he had "the coolest, clearest head, and best heart, and the exactest morals of almost any man I ever met with." Coleman acquired the

This drawing room in Woodford Mansion has been called by some authorities the loveliest in Colonial America.

property in 1756 and enlarged an earlier house. Later the King's collector of the port and the Crown agent, David Franks, lived here.

Woodford now houses the superb Naomi Wood collection of Colonial furniture and "household gear."

37

BELMONT MANSION

(*Map IV-A3*)

This was the home of the Peters family, particularly of Richard Peters who was commissioner of war during the Revolution and later a judge appointed by President Washington. Visitors may still see a date stone, 1745. From Belmont's lawns there is a magnificent view across the Schuylkill to the downtown city.

CEDAR GROVE (*Map IV-B4*)

Originally a Quaker country house on the old Frankford Road, Cedar Grove and its fine furnishings have been kept intact for more than two centuries.

The house was transported, stone by stone, to its present site in Fairmount Park, together with furnishings that had been handed down through generation after generation of family ownership.

SWEETBRIER

(Map IV-B4)

This fine house was the home of Samuel Breck. It was built in 1797. In its beautiful south parlor Breck entertained many distinguished guests, both American and French. Breck wrote the delightful book "Recollections" which gives an entertaining picture of his life and times.

STRAWBERRY MANSION

(Map IV-B2)

The first house on this site was owned by Charles Thomson, secretary of the Continental Congress. It was burned by British troops searching for Congressional records. The present mansion was started in 1797 by Judge William Lewis. It gets its name from exceptionally fine strawberry plants imported and cultivated by one of the early occupants. Pictured above is the handsome music room.

MOUNT PLEASANT
(*Map IV-B3*)

John Macpherson, a Scottish sea captain who made a fortune in privateering, built this mansion in 1761-62. It was called "the most elegant country seat in Pennsylvania" by John Adams when he visited in 1775. During the Revolution it was the residence of the Spanish minister. Benedict Arnold purchased it but never occupied it. (p. 79) The room shown below is the second-floor "great chamber."

CITY OF BENJAMIN FRANKLIN

Franklin Statue at Franklin Institute   *(Map I-A2)*

Benjamin Franklin's monument is not at the nation's capital in Washington but here in his own city where Franklin was—and still continues to be—the greatest of all Philadelphians.

In this city, Franklin is not merely a historic figure of the past; he continues to be very much a part of modern Philadelphia. Half-a-dozen or more institutions and organizations founded by Franklin still function today.

Franklin came to Philadelphia at the age of seventeen, already experienced in the printing trade after five years of apprenticeship. At the age of twenty-two he established his own business which earned him a fortune by the time he was in his early forties. He lived another forty years—a philosopher, scientist, statesman, public servant, and the world's best-known American.

The principal memorial to Franklin is beautiful Franklin Hall in the Franklin Institute on Philadelphia's Benjamin Franklin Parkway. (*Map I-A2*)

The building itself illustrates Franklin's many contributions to his community. When he died in 1790, his will left a trust fund to the city of Philadelphia. At the end of one hundred years, part of the trust, plus its accumulated earnings, was to be used for the benefit of the city; the remainder was to continue in trust for another hundred years, or until 1990.

When the first hundred years had ended, part of the Franklin trust was added to money from other sources and used to build the present home of the Franklin Institute. The remainder of the fund continues in trust, pending final distribution of Franklin's estate in 1990.

The Printer's Own Composing Stick at Franklin Institute

FRANKLIN
AS A
YOUNG MAN

Franklin's first arrival in Philadelphia as a tired, hungry, and poor young man is well portrayed by this statue on the campus of the University of Pennsylvania (*Map III-B3*), one of the institutions Franklin founded.

A treasure of Franklin's youth was a book *Logic, or the Art of Thinking,* which he read when he was about sixteen. It guided him throughout his life. He presented his copy of the book to the library which he founded. It is still in the possession of the Library Company, along with other Franklin volumes.

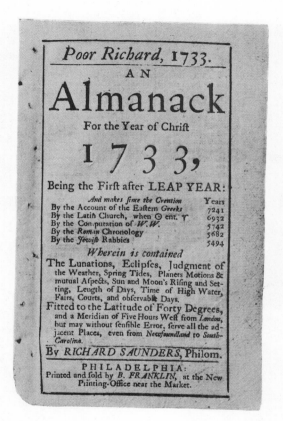

Poor Richard, 1733.

AN

Almanack

For the Year of Chrift

1733,

Being the Firft after LEAP YEAR:

And makes fince the Creation	Years
By the Account of the Eaftern *Greeks*	7241
By the Latin Church, when ☉ ent. ♈	6932
By the Computation of *W.W.*	5742
By the *Roman* Chronology	5682
By the *Jewish* Rabbies	5494

Wherein is contained

The Lunations, Eclipfes, Judgment of the Weather, Spring Tides, Planets Motions & mutual Afpects, Sun and Moon's Rifing and Setting, Length of Days, Time of High Water, Fairs, Courts, and obfervable Days.

Fitted to the Latitude of Forty Degrees, and a Meridian of Five Hours Weft from *London,* but may without fenfible Error, ferve all the adjacent Places, even from *Newfoundland* to *South-Carolina.*

By *RICHARD SAUNDERS*, Philom.

PHILADELPHIA:
Printed and fold by *B. FRANKLIN*, at the New Printing-Office near the Market.

As a printer, the young Franklin was industrious. He published pamphlets and books. He purchased a run-down newspaper, the *Pennsylvania Gazette,* and built it into the largest in the colonies. His greatest financial success was as publisher of *Poor Richard's Almanack*. This is the title page of the first issue published late in 1732 for the year 1733. Only one copy of the first printing is known to be in existence. It is available to scholars at the Rosenbach Foundation Philadelphia. (*Map I-A3*)

The old print below shows the home of Benjamin Franklin's Library Company of Philadelphia built in 1789. At the right is the reconstruction on the same site, now housing the Library of the American Philosophical Society.

BENJAMIN FRANKLIN'S LIBRARY

At the age of twenty-one, Franklin and a group of his friends formed "a club of mutual improvement" for purposes of writing and discussion. It was called the Junto. Four years later, in 1731, Franklin proposed formation of a library and persuaded fifty

The Cornerstone

The Order Box

friends, many of them Junto members, to pool their contributions for purchase of books in England.

The library imported its first books in 1732. It was later incorporated as The Library Company of Philadelphia, and is still in existence. At its headquarters may be seen some of the early minutes written by Franklin as secretary, and the original metal box in which members deposited requests for books to be imported.

The year before Franklin's death, the Library Company built a handsome brick building across 5th Street from the State House. Franklin wrote one of his typical inscriptions for the cornerstone, which is still preserved.

Although the original building was demolished in the 1880's, in

Franklin's Minutes

recent years another Franklin-founded institution, the American Philosophical Society, has built its own library in the same style and on the same site. (*Map I-D2*)

Since 1878 the Library Company has occupied the Ridgway building at Broad and Christian Streets. (*Map III-B3*)

Present Home of Franklin's Library

AMERICAN PHILOSOPHICAL SOCIETY (*Map I-D2*)

Philosophical Hall is the only private building in Independence Square. It is the headquarters of "The American Philosophical Society, held at Philadelphia, for Promoting Useful Knowledge." The Society was founded by Franklin in 1743 and for two centuries has played an important role in the cultural life of the country.

Franklin was thirty-seven and his printing business was flourishing when he proposed "That One Society be formed of Virtuosi or ingenious Men residing in the sev-eral Colonies to be called 'The American Philosophical Society' who are to maintain a constant Correspondence." Franklin served as president throughout the last twenty years of his life, during which time Philosophical Hall was built. The American Philosophical Society not only is still active, but also is the repository of many historic documents and treasures.

Across 5th Street from Philosophical Hall is the Society's library, which houses one of the most extensive collections of Franklin manuscripts in the world.

FRANKLIN'S HOSPITAL
(*Map I-C3*)

Franklin was instrumental in the founding of Pennsylvania Hospital in Philadelphia in 1751. It was the first hospital in America and is still flourishing.

Dr. Thomas Bond conceived the idea of the hospital, and appealed to Franklin for help in financing it. Franklin gave generously himself; he organized a group of contributors; and he worked out a unique arrangement for a matching appropriation from the Provincial Assembly. Franklin was first clerk or secretary of the board of managers, and he was the author of the engaging inscription carved on the hospital cornerstone.

Pennsylvania Hospital still occupies its original site and uses—along with other buildings—the original hospital structure which appears today much as it did more than two hundred years ago. Pennsylvania Hospital has been the scene of numerous "firsts" in American medicine.

Cornerstone Inscription

IN THE YEAR OF CHRIST
1755
GEORGE THE SECOND HAPPILY REIGNING;
(FOR HE SOUGHT THE HAPPINESS OF HIS PEOPLE)
PHILADELPHIA FLOURISHING,
(FOR ITS INHABITANTS WERE PUBLICK-SPIRITED)
THIS BUILDING,
BY THE BOUNTY OF THE GOVERNMENT,
AND OF MANY PRIVATE PERSONS
WAS PIOUSLY FOUNDED,
FOR THE RELIEF OF THE SICK AND MISERABLE.
MAY THE GOD OF MERCIES
BLESS THE UNDERTAKING!

FRANKLIN'S FIRE INSURANCE COMPANY

Franklin was one of the directors who helped found, in 1752, what is now the oldest insurance company in America. He published its notices in his newspaper and printed its policies in his printshop. The company is the Philadelphia Contributionship for the Insurance of Houses From Loss by Fire. (*Map I-D3*) The company is also called "Hand-in-Hand" from its old fire mark which may still be seen on many houses in Philadelphia and suburbs. Today the company is housed in a handsome old building on 4th Street where visitors may sign the register with a quill pen and may see the parchment scroll signed by its early policyholders. Franklin's name heads the list.

PERSONAL MEMENTOS OF FRANKLIN

Franklin's clock owned by the American Philosophical Society. (Map I-D2)

His desk at the University of Pennsylvania. (Map III-B3)

The hand-cranked electrostatic generator which Franklin used in his experiments with electricity, the most famous of which was the kite. On exhibit at Franklin Institute. (Map I-A2)

The library chair (with folding steps) which Franklin invented and used during his later years. Owned by the American Philosophical Society. (Map I-D2)

FRANKLIN'S UNIVERSITY   (*Map III-B3*)

Benjamin Franklin was also the founder of the University of Pennsylvania. His *Proposals relating to the Education of Youth in Pennsylvania* provided the necessary impetus which transformed the "Charity School," established in 1740, into the "College, and Academy, and Charitable School of Philadelphia."

Franklin was first president of the trustees of the academy which became the University of Pennsylvania in 1791.

Since 1872 the university campus has been located in West Philadel-

Academy Bell—*At one time this bell rang for both the Academy and the Union Fire Company, which Franklin founded and which was located nearby. The bell is now on exhibition at the University library.*

phia. One of the city's great urban redevelopment programs is now centered around this area.

The athletic stadium at the university is named Franklin Field in honor of the founder.

LIFELONG PUBLIC SERVANT

Night Watchman's Box
Friends Meeting House
Fourth and Arch Streets

Franklin devoted himself to public service throughout his life. He served as Philadelphia alderman and city councilman. He organized a night watch to protect citizens and their homes. He drew up the first plan for paving the city streets.

Franklin was clerk and later a member of the Pennsylvania Assembly for many years. He was postmaster for the province and, afterwards, for all of America. He spent some fifteen years in England as agent for Pennsylvania.

In contrast to the many young men of the American Revolution, Franklin was seventy years old when he served in the Continental Congress and as a member of the Committee of Five which drafted the Declaration of Independence. He went to Paris as agent of Congress and negotiated the all-important alliance with France. Later he was minister to France.

At the age of eighty-one Franklin was the elder statesman of the Constitutional Convention. He was the author of the principal compromise which led to the adoption of the Constitution. Finally, he was elected to three terms as president of the executive council of Pennsylvania, retiring just before he died at age eighty-four.

FRANKLIN'S WILL—AND HIS GRAVE

Franklin's will, leaving a trust fund to the city of Philadelphia, is on loan to the American Philosophical Society and is on exhibition at its library. (*Map I-D2*) In his will, Franklin first called himself printer, and then minister plenipotentiary and president of Pennsylvania. He described in detail the plain stone to be placed over his grave. Franklin is buried in the burial ground of Christ Church, 5th and Arch Streets. (*Map I-D2*) At the time of his death this was in the "suburbs." In recent years it has become customary for visitors to place pennies on Franklin's grave out of respect and affection for "Poor Richard."

CITY OF INDEPENDENCE

As tension developed between the American colonies and Great Britain, Philadelphia became a focal point of organized opposition to British colonial policy.

The city successfully defied the Stamp Act passed by Parliament in 1765. When the ship *Royal Charlotte* brought the first stamps and stamped paper to Philadelphia, a mass meeting was held in the Pennsylvania State House; the resignation of the stamp commissioner was demanded; merchants resolved to import no more English goods until the tax was repealed; and newspapers announced they would suspend publication rather than submit to the tax.

The stamps intended for Philadelphia were never used. They went back to England on the same ship which brought them. At the Library Company of Philadelphia (*Map III-B3*) this issue of the *Pennsylvania Journal* for October 31, 1765 tells the story of Philadelphia resistance.

THE PHILADELPHIA TEA PARTY

Philadelphia also led opposition to the British tax on tea, holding a "Tea Party" that was less spectacular than, but just as effective as, the one in Boston.

In September, 1773, word was received in America that the first tea shipments were on their way. Philadelphians held a town meeting at the State House on October 17 and adopted eight resolutions. One declared: "that the duty imposed by Parliament upon tea landed in America is a tax on the Americans, or levying contributions on them without their consent."

In Boston three weeks later, a meeting in Faneuil Hall resolved: "the sense of this town cannot be better expressed, than in the words of certain judicious resolves, lately entered into by our worthy brethren the citizens of Philadelphia."

The tea shipment for Boston was the first to arrive, and the cargo was dumped into the harbor there on December 16. On Christmas Day, the ship *Polly* bound for Philadelphia arrived in the Delaware River. Pilots stopped her at Gloucester, New Jersey, below the city, and her master, Captain Ayres, was escorted overland to Philadelphia by a citizens committee. On December 27 he was taken to attend a mass meeting of 8000 Philadelphians in the State House yard. It was the largest crowd ever assembled in the colonies. A number of resolutions were adopted, the first being "that the tea . . . shall not be landed."

The crowd was orderly, but determined. Captain Ayres was convinced. He agreed to sail his ship back home, was given two days to provision her, and then returned to England without any of his cargo being unloaded.

The *Polly* carried, in addition to its cargo of tea, a new bell cast in England for the tower of Germantown Academy. (p. 23) The bell went back across the ocean with the rest of the unloaded cargo. It was delivered years later, and now hangs in the Academy tower. The British crown may be seen on the tower. (*Map III-B2*)

CARPENTERS' HALL

(Map I-D2)

Paul Revere made several historic rides from Boston to Philadelphia long before his shorter gallop in 1775, to Lexington and Concord, which made him famous. He was the courier who carried news of Boston's tea party to New York and Philadelphia in 1773. He made the long trip again in May, 1774, with word that the British had closed the port of Boston. This brought to a head the growing sentiment for "a Congress of Delegates from all the Colonies." On September 5, 1774, the First Continental Congress met in Philadelphia. The delegates assembled first at the "genteel and elegant" City Tavern now being restored. They were offered the use of the Pennsylvania State House for their formal sessions. Instead they chose to meet in a nearby building which had just been completed by the Carpenters' Company.

Carpenters' Hall was a Colonial version of a guildhall, the headquarters of the master craftsmen who were also the builders and architects of early America. The Carpenters' Company continues as an active organization, and still uses its venerable hall.

FIRST CONTINENTAL CONGRESS

The delegates to the First Continental Congress were men of ability and prominence in their respective colonies. George Washington and John Adams were among them, but at that time were not as widely known as two of their colleagues, Samuel Adams and Patrick Henry. Benjamin Franklin was in England, in 1774, as agent for the Pennsylvania Assembly and did not attend. Peyton Randolph, leader of the Virginia delegation, was chosen president of the Congress.

Despite their variety of religious affiliations, the delegates invited a clergyman from Christ Church, Jacob Duché, to offer the first prayer. A print of this scene is in the collection of the Independence National Historical Park. Duché was later elected chaplain of Congress.

As its secretary, the Congress chose a Philadelphian, Charles Thomson, a remarkable man who played an important part in the Revolution but is not at all well-known in American history.

At first, the Congress considered a Plan of Union setting up an American legislature to exercise joint control with Parliament. This was voted down. The Congress then adopted a Declaration of Rights and Grievances, written by delegate John Dickinson, a Philadelphia lawyer. It also adopted the Association, pledging colonists not to use British goods nor to trade with Britain until their rights were recognized.

The Congress adjourned on October 26, 1774. It resolved that another Congress should be held in Philadelphia the next May "unless the redress of grievances, which we have desired, be obtained before that time."

THE SECRETARY OF CONGRESS

Charles Thomson of Philadelphia, secretary of the Continental Congress, was a forty-five-year-old former schoolmaster turned businessman. He was not a delegate, but as a member of the Pennsylvania Assembly had helped make arrangements for the Congress. He continued to serve as secretary throughout the Revolutionary period. His signature appears on both the Declaration of Independence and the Constitution of the United States.

Thomson lived first in a fine home overlooking the Schuylkill. (p. 40) After retirement from public life, he occupied the estate which had been Mrs. Thomson's family home. This had been built in 1704 in the "Welsh Tract" laid out by William Penn. The original name of the estate was "Bryn Mawr" (from which the present Main Line community takes its name). The place later was renamed "Harriton." The house is still standing. (*Map II-B2*)

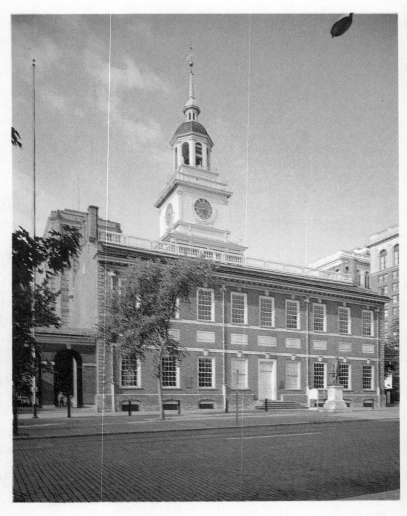

Independence Hall (The Pennsylvania State House) (*Map I-D2*)

SECOND CONTINENTAL CONGRESS

The Second Continental Congress met in Philadelphia on May 10, 1775, and sat in the meeting room of the provincial assembly in the Pennsylvania State House—now known as Independence Hall.

There had already been fighting between minutemen and British redcoats at Lexington and Concord in April. Large numbers of militiamen had gathered around Boston. Although Congress sent a conciliatory address to the King, it proceeded to organize the American Continental Army and in June named the Virginia delegate, George Washington, to take charge. He proceeded to Massachusetts and took command at Cambridge.

Toward the end of 1775, Congress established the Navy and the Marine Corps. Esek Hopkins, of Rhode Island, was first commodore of the Navy. One of the captains was a youthful Philadelphia shipmaster, John Barry, who brought into the city in April, 1776, the first captured British vessel. After the Revolution he became known as "Father of the United States Navy." His statue stands in the center of Independence Square. One of the Navy's first lieutenants was John Paul Jones, hero of daring exploits, whose grave is at Annapolis.

The first commandant of the Marines was a young Philadelphian, Samuel Nicholas. He set up his headquarters in Tun Tavern (*Map I-D2*) near the waterfront. A Marine Corps museum is now housed in New Hall, near Carpenters' Hall. (*Map I-D2*)

A RESOLUTION FOR INDEPENDENCE

By 1776, the demand for independence was swelling throughout the colonies. The pamphlet "Common Sense" written by the Philadelphia editor, Thomas Paine, played an important part. In April, North Carolina authorized its delegates in Congress to vote for independence, and in May, the Virginia delegation was so instructed.

On June 7, Richard Henry Lee of Virginia, offered a resolution: "that these United colonies are, and of right ought to be, free and independent States . . ." There were two days of discussion; Congress postponed action for three weeks—until July 1—". . . and in the meanwhile, that no time be lost, in case the Congress agree thereto, a committee be appointed to prepare a declaration."

THE DECLARATION OF INDEPENDENCE

Congress named a committee of five to draw up the Declaration of Independence. That group, in turn, entrusted the first draft to thirty-three-year-old Thomas Jefferson of Virginia. While in Philadelphia, he was renting rooms in a house on the southwest corner of 7th and Market Streets (*Map I-C2*) and there, during three weeks in June, 1776, he wrote the most famous of all American documents.

The American Philosophical Society (*Map I-D2*) owns a draft of the Declaration in Jefferson's own handwriting which shows changes in wording suggested by two other members of the drafting committee, Benjamin Franklin and John Adams. The Society also owns a chair in which Jefferson is said to have sat while writing.

The Declaration was completed and reported to Congress on June 28, 1776. On July 1, the delegates resumed consideration of Lee's resolution for independence and adopted it the next day. John Adams wrote that July 2 would go down in history as American Independence Day.

On Thursday, July 4, Congress adopted the Declaration of Independence as a justification for the Resolution of July 2. Congress ordered that the Declaration be printed, and turned at once to other business. There were no ceremonies or celebrations that day.

On Monday, July 8, the Declaration was proclaimed to a crowd in the State House yard at noon, being read by John Nixon, a member of the Committee of Safety. On July 19, Congress ordered that an official copy be engrossed on parchment, and this copy finally was signed by Congress on August 2, 1776. This signed Declaration is now in Washington.

Celebration of the Fourth of July as Independence Day began the next year when Congress arranged a dinner for prominent Philadelphians on that date.

Jefferson's Writing Chair

a Declaration by the Representatives of the UNITED STATES OF AMERICA in General Congress assembled

When in the course of human events it becomes necessary for one people to dissolve the political bands which have connected them with another, and to assume among the powers of the earth the separate and equal station to which the laws of nature & of nature's god entitle them, a decent respect to the opinions of mankind requires that they should declare the causes which impel them to the separation

We hold these truths to be self evident, that all men are created equal; that they are endowed by their creator with inherent and unalienable rights, that among these are life, liberty, & the pursuit of happiness; that to secure these rights, governments are instituted among men, deriving their just powers from the consent of the governed; that whenever any form of government becomes destructive of these ends, it is the right of the people to alter or to abolish it, and to institute new government, laying it's foundation on such principles and organising it's powers in such form as to them shall seem most likely to effect their safety and happiness. prudence indeed will dictate that governments long established should not be changed for light & transient causes; and accordingly all experience hath shewn that mankind are more disposed to suffer, while evils are sufferable than to right themselves by abolishing the forms to which they are accustomed. but when a long train of abuses and usurpations, begun at a distinguished period & pursuing invariably the same object evinces a design to reduce them under absolute despotism, it is their right, it is their duty, to throw off such government, & to provide new guards for their future security. such has been the patient sufferance of these colonies; & such is now the necessity which constrains them to expunge their former systems of government. the history of the present king of Great Britain, is a history of unremitting injuries and usurpations, among which appears no solitary fact to contradict the uniform tenor of the rest, but all have in direct object the establishment of an absolute tyranny over these states. to prove this let facts be submitted to a candid world, for the truth of which we pledge a faith yet unsullied by falsehood

He has refused his assent to laws the most wholesome and necessary for the public good.

he has forbidden his governors to pass laws of immediate & pressing importance, unless suspended in their operation till his assent should be obtained; and when so suspended, he has neglected utterly to attend to them.

he has refused to pass other laws for the accommodation of large districts of people, unless those people would relinquish the right of representation in the legislature; a right inestimable to them & formidable to tyrants only.

Draft of the Declaration in Jefferson's Hand

63

Congress Voting Independence

This famous painting by Edward Savage is at the Historical Society of Pennsylvania. (Map I-C3) It gives the most authentic concept of the events of July 4, 1776 and shows the assembly room as it appeared at that time. The room is now being restored.

Assembly Room
Independence Hall
(*Map I-D2*)

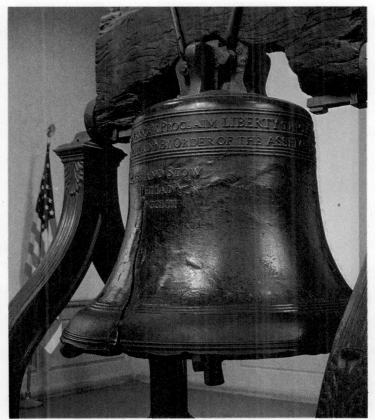

THE LIBERTY BELL

The most venerated symbol of freedom in America is on display at Independence Hall. (*Map I-D2*) It was hanging in the tower of the old building in July, 1776, when Independence was voted and proclaimed. The bell already bore its prophetic inscription: "Proclaim liberty throughout all the land . . ." (p. 14)

65

THE SILVER INKSTAND

In signing the Declaration of Independence, delegates to the Continental Congress used this handsome silver inkstand which the Pennsylvania assembly had purchased for the speaker's table when the State House was first furnished some twenty years earlier. This is now one of the historic treasures at Independence Hall.

"THE AMERICAN BELL"

A highlight of a summer visit to Philadelphia is the evening, outdoor performance of a sound-and-light drama called "The American Bell." Seated in the yard of Independence Hall where so many of America's historic figures played their parts, today's visitors can see and hear a stirring presentation of the events of the Revolution.

MEN BEHIND THE DECLARATION

John Hancock
President of the
Continental Congress
by S. F. B. Morse

Charles Thomson
Secretary of the
Continental Congress
by C. W. Peale

Richard Henry Lee
Proposer of the
Resolution for Independence
by C. W. Peale

Thomas Jefferson
Author of the
Declaration of Independence
by C. W. Peale

Independence National Historical Park owns a fine collection of portraits of men who played leading parts in the early days of the nation. Many of these are the work of Charles Willson Peale, who settled in Philadelphia in 1776 and became the best-known portrait painter in the colonies. In later life, Peale exhibited his paintings in a museum which was located for more than twenty-five years in the State House. (p. 114) The city of Philadelphia eventually purchased a substantial number of the Peale portraits and today they form an important part of the National Park collection.

WASHINGTON CROSSES THE DELAWARE

By December, 1776, the Continental Army had suffered serious defeats in New York and had retreated across New Jersey into Pennsylvania. British forces appeared to be sweeping triumphantly southward to capture Philadelphia. Congress moved to Baltimore.

Then, on the bitter cold Christmas night of 1776, George Washington and 2400 men recrossed the ice-filled Delaware River from the Pennsylvania side (*Map II-C1*), surprised the Hessian mercenaries employed by the British, and won the key battles of Trenton and Princeton. (*Map II-D1*) This bold stroke kept Philadelphia safe for the time being, and instilled new life into the Revolutionary effort.

Today there are state parks on both sides of the Delaware at what is known as Washington Crossing. A trip to this historic spot makes a pleasant day's outing for the family visiting Philadelphia.

HOUSE OF DECISION

This double farmhouse near the Delaware River, occupied by the Thompson and Neely families, served in December, 1776 as the headquarters of one of Washington's commanders, General Lord Stirling. Here General Washington held councils of war which led

to the decision to cross the river in open iron ore boats manned by a Massachusetts regiment that included fishermen and seamen from Marblehead.

This house is completely furnished in 18th century style and open to visitors. At the rear is a red cedar tree which was standing at the time of Washington's crossing. Near the house are buried twenty unknown Continental soldiers. Also nearby is the grave of a twenty-four-year-old captain who died of "camp fever" on Christmas Day in the temporary military hospital on the ground floor of the House of Decision.

Seventy-five years after Washington's military feat, this familiar painting was executed by the German-American painter, Emanuel Leutze. Given to the Metropolitan Museum of Art, New York City, by John S. Kennedy in 1897, it is on loan to the Washington Crossing State Park, Pennsylvania, and is housed in the auditorium of the memorial amphitheater near the edge of the Delaware.

POINT OF EMBARKATION

This monument beside the broad Delaware River is near the spot from which Washington and his men embarked on their crossing of the river. Nearby, in the Pennsylvania state park, are an observatory tower overlooking the Delaware Valley, a wild flower preserve with well-marked flower trails, and a large picnic area.

BETSY ROSS AND THE AMERICAN FLAG

On June 14, 1777, the Continental Congress resolved "that the Flag of the United States be thirteen stripes alternate red and white; that the Union be thirteen stars white in a blue field, representing a new constellation."

One of the most popular stories in American history is that a committee of Congress went to the home of the Philadelphia seamstress, Betsy Ross, and engaged her to make the first Stars and Stripes, she showing them with a snip of her scissors how to cut out a five-pointed star. A tiny Colonial house at 239 Arch Street, restored and furnished by patriotic groups, is visited by hundreds of thousands every year as "The Birthplace of Old Glory." (*Map I-D2*)

Not all of the Betsy Ross story can be documented, but there are enough facts to justify persistence of the popular legend. One record in Pennsylvania archives shows a payment on May 29, 1777, to Mrs. Elizabeth Ross "for making ship's Colours etc" for the Pennsylvania Navy. Other records show Betsy Ross made flags for the government for some fifty years after the Revolution. She died in 1836 and is buried in Mount Moriah cemetery, Philadelphia. (*Map III-A4*) The American flag always flies over her grave.

THE BRITISH CAPTURE PHILADELPHIA

Having failed to take Philadelphia in 1776, the British General Howe tried again in 1777. He was unable to force his way up the Delaware River so he sailed up Chesapeake Bay, then marched overland from the south. Washington's army tried to intercept him at Brandywine Creek, near Chadds Ford, Pennsylvania, some thirty-five miles from the city, but

Monument at Paoli (Map II-B2)

the Americans were soundly defeated in the Battle of Brandywine on September 11.

In this battle, the wealthy young French nobleman, Lafayette, was wounded. He had arrived in Philadelphia in July to offer his services, and Congress had made him a general. Another of Washington's generals was the daring "Mad Anthony" Wayne, whose family home, built in 1724, was only a few miles from the battleground. The house, called "Waynesborough," still stands. It contains a number of the general's possessions. (*Map II-B2*)

As the British moved slowly toward Philadelphia, there was sporadic fighting. On September 21 the enemy surprised and routed a small detachment of Wayne's men at night in a bloody engagement which became known as The Paoli Massacre. A park and monument mark the spot along Philadelphia's "Main Line." (*Map II-B2*)

Without further serious fighting, the British entered Philadelphia on September 26, 1777. Their first camp was in the Society Hill area. (*Map I-D3*)

The Continental Congress fled to Lancaster, and then to York, Pennsylvania. The Liberty Bell and the bells from Christ Church were taken to Allentown, and hidden beneath the floor of Zion Reformed Church.

Lafayette's Headquarters at Brandywine (Map II-A3)

THE BATTLE OF GERMANTOWN (*Map III-B2*)

Eight days after the British occupied Philadelphia, Washington attempted another surprise attack similar to his crossing of the Delaware the previous year. This resulted in the Battle of Germantown on October 4, 1777.

The British Commander, Howe, had established his quarters at Stenton, the James Logan Mansion. (p. 22) He had posted a three-mile line of troops to protect the city from the north, the line extending through the heart of Germantown. Washington pretended to fortify his camp in Worcester Township, north of Germantown, and then marched his men fourteen miles at night. He divided his force into four columns, each approaching by a different road to surprise the British line at dawn.

The plan was bold and at first successful. The British were thrown into confusion and began a major retreat. Then suddenly, the battle turned into an American defeat when in dense early-morning fog an American officer led his men between two of Washington's columns so that one group of American soldiers was firing upon another.

Washington was forced to order a general retreat. British reinforcements arrived. Howe was able to strengthen and maintain his hold upon the principal city of the colonies.

THE CHEW HOUSE
  (*Map III-B1*)

A dramatic incident in the Battle of Germantown centered around Cliveden, the handsome stone house built in 1761 by Benjamin Chew, Chief Justice of the province of Pennsylvania. During the British retreat, a British colonel leading 120 men entered the Chew House and barricaded it.

The first wave of American troops passed by the house and continued in pursuit of the enemy. Later, Washington and his staff arrived on the scene. They halted in front of what is now known as the Billmeyer House, the nearest house to the Chew mansion. Washington surveyed the situation through a field glass, and ordered that the British be dislodged from the Chew House by the American reserve forces.

A young lieutenant from Virginia, carrying a flag of truce, was sent to demand surrender. He was shot and killed as he crossed the

*The Chew
House Today*

*Chew House During the
Battle of Germantown*

lawn. American artillery then began bombarding the house, and several brave men charged the walls in efforts to set the place on fire. The stone mansion withstood all attacks. The Chew House was still in enemy hands when the tide of battle turned. Members of the Chew family still live in the historic house.

The Billmeyer House

73

THE BATTLE OF FORT MIFFLIN

(Map III-B4)

The situation of the British in Philadelphia was at first precarious. Washington's army cut off the flow of supplies by land; the Delaware River was effectively blocked against British ships; food grew scarce; British soldiers burned fences and church pews for firewood; and wounded soldiers and prisoners suffered great hardships.

The river was guarded by a few American warships, by floating gun batteries, and by rows of iron-pointed timbers strung from shore to shore. The most effective defenses, however, were two forts— Fort Mercer on the New Jersey side and what is now known as Fort Mifflin on the Pennsylvania shore.

In order to open a supply route for their bottled-up army, British land and naval forces opened a day-and-night attack on Fort Mifflin on November 10, 1777. The old fort was subjected to intense bombardment. By November 16, it was a ruin, its guns out of action, and 250 men killed or wounded. The defenders did not surrender, however, but successfully evacuated the fort, taking their wounded with them.

Fort Mifflin was rebuilt in 1798 and still stands. Near it may be seen "Cannonball House" a brick

residence built by Swedish settlers as early as 1660. Its walls were pierced by shot during the battle.

The British succeeded in opening the river, and thereafter enjoyed a winter of comfort, sometimes even luxury in Philadelphia while the Continental army suffered in camp.

DAWESFIELD

After the Battle of Germantown, Washington's army remained north of Philadelphia in Whitemarsh Valley (*Map II-C2*), and the general made his headquarters at a number of country houses. For twelve days he was at Dawesfield, built fifty years earlier, and in 1777 the home of James and Elizabeth Dawes Morris. It is still owned and occupied by members of the same family, passing from generation to generation through the distaff side. It is open to visitors by appointment.

Washington established headquarters at Dawesfield on October 21, 1777. Here he and his generals rejoiced over news of the American victory at Saratoga, where the British General Burgoyne surrendered with his entire army. This success enabled Benjamin Franklin, in Paris, to obtain a formal alliance with France.

In the parlor of Dawesfield, a court-martial of General Anthony Wayne was held at his request to investigate charges that he was to blame for the disaster at Paoli. Wayne was acquitted, and the court honored him for bravery.

Washington used one of the upstairs bedrooms of this house. The four-poster in which he slept is still in the room. A first-floor room immediately below this one was used by Lafayette, who could not climb stairs because of a wound suffered at Brandywine.

Washington left Dawesfield on November 2, 1777.

VALLEY FORGE

(*Map II-B2*)

Valley Forge has become a symbol of the hardships endured by American patriots. But this was not a battlefield; it was the camping ground of the cold, ragged, hungry Continental army during the winter of 1777-78 while the British were in Philadelphia.

The once-cheerless hills and fields of Valley Forge are now a state park. A one-day trip to this historic ground should be part of every family's visit to Philadelphia. It is particularly beautiful in spring, with thousands of dogwood trees in bloom.

Washington and his generals made their headquarters in farmhouses and country residences, while other officers and men lived in log huts. Some of the houses remain, and a number of huts have been reproduced.

Adjacent to the park is the Washington Memorial Chapel with its celebrated stained-glass windows and carvings. A stone bell tower houses a carillon which is played at intervals during the day.

Adjoining the chapel is a museum maintained by the Valley Forge Historical Society.

WASHINGTON'S HEADQUARTERS

At Valley Forge, Washington occupied the stone house owned by Isaac Potts, son of the ironmaster of the nearby forge which gave the area its name. The house is now furnished with relics of Washington's occupancy.

It was Potts who later told the story of how one day he came upon Washington's horse tied to a sapling, and in a thicket he saw the General on his knees praying fervently.

There was one great occasion at Valley Forge when news of the alliance with France was received. Washington ordered an entire day of celebration beginning early in the morning with prayer and ending with cannonading and musket fire at night.

Valley Forge Chapel

André, Benedict Arnold and the Philadelphia Tories

The British occupied Philadelphia for nine months. Although many patriot families had fled the city, numerous Tory families remained. They were wealthy for the most part and they entertained British officers lavishly.

One fashionable Tory household was that of Judge Edward Shippen. He and his wife and their daughters frequently had at their home one particular officer, the artistic and talented young John André.

When the British commander Howe resigned and was replaced by General Clinton in May, 1778, Major André arranged an extravagant pageant and ball called "The Meschianza" in Howe's honor.

Ticket to the British Officers' Meschianza

Many Tory young ladies were invited, among them three Edward Shippen daughters. The Meschianza included a regatta, a military procession, a jousting tournament in which British officers and Tory belles played the parts of knights and their ladies, and dancing until 4 A.M. The affair was so elaborate it has been written up at length in Philadelphia histories. Major André conceived and staged the Meschianza; designed costumes and hair styles for the ladies; and painted scenery and decorations.

A month after the Meschianza, on June 18, 1778, the British evacuated Philadelphia. The Americans moved in the same day, and while the main army pursued the British northward, American Gen-

Meschianza Procession

eral Benedict Arnold was made military governor of the city.

Arnold had been a heroic soldier, but a controversial figure. As commander of the city he lived lavishly and preferred the society of the same Tories who had befriended the British. Within a few months, the thirty-seven-year-old Arnold married Judge Shippen's eighteen-year-old daughter, Peggy. He bought an elegant mansion for her (p. 41) but his fortunes were changing, and neither he nor his bride ever lived there.

Arnold was accused of using his military position to enrich himself. Congress ordered him to trial and he was convicted but only reprimanded. Thereafter, he was made

American commander at West Point. When he treacherously offered to deliver that fort to the enemy, the British officer designated to negotiate with him was John André, the old friend of Arnold's bride and other Philadelphia Tories.

The conspiracy was discovered. Arnold fled to the British, served for awhile in their army, then went to live in England where his young Philadelphia wife joined him. Major André, however, was captured inside the American lines with evidence in his possession. He was hanged. Just before his death, the talented officer made one more drawing—a sketch of himself awaiting execution.

LAST YEARS OF THE WAR

Philadelphia again became the capital of the Revolution after the British withdrew. Congress returned to the assembly room in the State House in July, 1778, and found the building in "a most filthy and sordid situation." It had been used as a barracks, a prison, and a hospital during British occupation.

On July 9, 1778, eight states signed the new Articles of Confederation which finally became effective in 1781.

During the last years of the Revolution, major fighting was in the south. The war ended, for practical purposes, on October 19, 1781 when Washington and the French General Rochambeau trapped Lord Cornwallis and his army on the peninsula at Yorktown while the French fleet held off reinforcements.

Unofficial word of Cornwallis's surrender was brought to Philadelphia by an express-rider who reached the city at 3 A.M. on October 22. A night watchman shouted the news to the populace as he made his rounds. Two days later, Washington's official dispatch was brought by his aide, Colonel Tilghman, a Philadelphian. Congress attended services of thanksgiving at the Dutch Reformed Church and at St. Mary's.

On Saturday, November 3, 1781, twenty-four captured battle flags of Cornwallis's army were brought to Philadelphia, paraded through the streets, and formally presented to Congress at the State House.

Peace negotiations were begun in 1782 in Paris, the American commissioners being Benjamin Franklin, John Jay, and John

Adams. The treaty was concluded in 1783 and finally ratified by Congress in Philadelphia on January 14, 1784.

THE UNKNOWN SOLDIER OF THE REVOLUTION (*Map I-C3*)

This monument in Washington Square, Philadelphia marks the tomb of the unknown soldier of the Revolution. It is a memorial to all who died to establish American freedom.

Near Washington Square were the city jail, which the British used as a military prison, and the State House, which served both as hospital and as prison. An uncounted number of unfortunate Continental soldiers who died in these buildings were unceremoniously buried in common graves in this Square. No more fitting place could be found for the nation's monument to them.

CITY OF THE CONSTITUTION

The Constitution of the United States was drawn up and adopted in Philadelphia in the same building and in the same room as the Declaration of Independence.

The need for a new and strong national government had been widely recognized. The Articles of Confederation were inadequate. Congress lacked authority to transact public business effectively, even after the Revolution ended. Washington, as early as 1783, urged a stronger federal government.

THE AMERICAN "EMPIRE"

This date stone on the Free Quaker Meeting House at 5th and Arch Streets (*Map I-D2*) illustrates the uncertainty and confusion about the American form of government after the Declaration of Independence in 1776. It refers to 1783 as the eighth year of "the empire."

The Free Quakers were Friends who supported the Revolution and in many cases fought with the Continental Army. Their Meeting House is now being restored.

THE CONSTITUTIONAL CONVENTION

Congress called a Constitutional convention "for the sole and express purpose of revising the Articles of Confederation." But the convention delegates took upon themselves the task of forming a wholly new government.

The convention was to have assembled on May 14, 1787. Delegates were slow to arrive in Philadelphia, however, and it was not until May 25 that meetings began. Washington was unanimously elected president of the convention. There were fifty-five delegates from twelve states (none from Rhode Island). The convention decided its work should be done in private. No minutes were kept; no one attended the sessions except members. George Washington even discontinued his personal diary for the period of the convention. Historians must trace its proceedings through a few journals, principally one kept by James Madison.

Throughout a hot and humid Philadelphia summer, the delegates met at the State House five and six hours a day, six days a week. They were an able and dis-

James Madison
"Father of the Constitution"

James Wilson
Author of the First Draft

tinguished group of men. Although they had sincere and intense differences of opinion, they reached workable compromises on all important issues. The first draft of the Constitution was written by Philadelphia lawyer James Wilson, and is still preserved at the Historical Society of Pennsylvania. (*Map I-C3*)

On Saturday, September 15, 1787, the convention reached agreement and adjourned over the weekend for the final draft to be printed. Monday, September 17, the delegates met to vote. Benjamin Franklin, ill and feeble at the age of eighty-one, wrote out a fervent appeal for unanimity which was read for him by Wilson. This speech eventually was printed and became the best-known record of the convention.

Franklin's Speech on the Constitution

September 17, 1787

"I confess that there are several parts of this Constitution which I do not at present approve, but I am not sure I shall never approve them; for, having lived long, I have experienced many instances of being obliged by better information or fuller consideration to change opinions, even on important subjects, which I once thought right, but found to be otherwise. It is therefore that the older I grow the more apt I am to doubt my own judgment and to pay more respect to the judgment of others . . .

"I doubt too whether any other convention we can obtain may be able to make a better Constitution. For when you assemble a number of men to have the advantage of their joint wisdom, you inevitably assemble with those men all their prejudices, their passions, their errors of opinion, their local interests, and their selfish views. From such an assembly can a perfect production be expected? It therefore astonishes me, Sir, to find this system approaching so near to perfection as it does . . .

"Thus, I consent, Sir, to this Constitution because I expect no better, and because I am not sure that it is not the best . . . On the whole, Sir, I cannot help expressing a wish that every member of the convention who may still have objections to it would, with me, on this occasion doubt a little of his own infallibility and, to make manifest our unanimity put his name to this instrument."

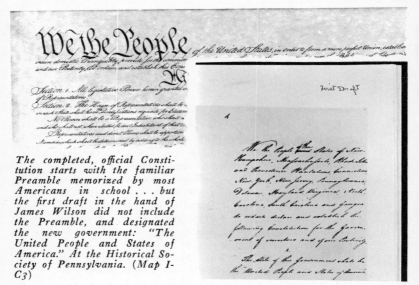

The completed, official Constitution starts with the familiar Preamble memorized by most Americans in school . . . but the first draft in the hand of James Wilson did not include the Preamble, and designated the new government: "The United People and States of America." At the Historical Society of Pennsylvania. (Map I-C3)

ADOPTION OF THE CONSTITUTION

When debate on the Constitution was concluded, Franklin moved that it be signed as "done in Convention by the unanimous consent of the states present," this language being carefully chosen in view of the fact that Rhode Island was not represented and some individual delegates of other states were not willing to sign. The document was signed by thirty-nine delegates to become effective upon ratification by nine of the states.

Delaware was the first to rat-ify, thus earning its place as "The First State." Pennsylvania followed five days later, and New Jersey six days after that. The Constitution became effective when the ninth state ratified it on June 21, 1788. Eleven states had approved by the time Washington was inaugurated the first President of the United States on April 30, 1789. The twelfth and thirteenth states ratified the Constitution after the new government had been installed.

THE RISING SUN

While delegates to the convention were signing the completed Constitution on September 17, 1787, according to Madison's journal, the aged Benjamin Franklin called attention to the President's chair which Washington had occupied all through four months of difficult deliberations.

Said Franklin: "I have often and often in the course of the session and the vicissitudes of my hopes and fears as to its issue, looked at that behind the President without being able to tell whether it was rising or setting. But now at length I have the happiness to know that it is a rising and not a setting sun."

CAPITAL OF THE UNITED STATES

The first capital of the United States under the new Constitution was New York City. However, the First Congress decided that the permanent capital would be a new federal city on the Potomac, and that while the city of Washington was being built, the capital would be Philadelphia.

On December 6, 1790, the First Congress met in Philadelphia, and this continued to be the capital city for the next ten years. At that time, two buildings adjoining the State House had just been completed. The building to the west, at the corner of 6th and Chestnut Streets, had been built as the Philadelphia County Court House. It was turned over to the Federal Government for the use of Congress, and has been known since as Congress Hall. (*Map I-C2*)

The House of Representatives sat in the large room on the first floor of Congress Hall. The United States Senate met in a room on the second floor. This is where Washington was inaugurated for his second term, and where he delivered his last message to Congress in 1796. (This was not Washington's "Farewell Address," which actually was written while Congress was in recess and published in a Philadelphia newspaper, the *Daily Advertiser.* One of Philadelphia's newspapers today is the *Inquirer,* successor to the *Advertiser,* and the oldest daily newspaper in the United States.)

The new building to the east of the State House at 5th and Chestnut Streets (*Map I-D2*) had been intended for use as the Philadelphia City Hall. Here the United States Supreme Court sat.

Philadelphia was still the capital when John Adams, vice-president under Washington, was elected second President of the United States. Adams took the oath of office in the House of Representatives in Congress Hall, on March 4, 1797. Two years later, Congress assembled there to receive official news of Washington's death at Mount Vernon. The members heard repeated the famous words "First in war; first in peace; first in the hearts of his countrymen" which General Lee had used in his funeral oration in Philadelphia's Old Zion Lutheran Church. The church was located at 4th and Cherry Streets. (*Map I-D2*) The old building is gone, but the church still exists as St. Michael-Zion German Lutheran Church, Franklin Street above Race. (*Map I-C1*)

THREE PRESIDENTIAL MANSIONS

THE ROBERT MORRIS HOUSE (*Map I-D2*)

While the Constitutional convention was in session, George Washington lived in a house on Market Street west of 5th, owned by his friend Robert Morris. When he returned to Philadelphia as President, he occupied the same house and lived there throughout his term of office. The house has since been demolished, but old drawings of it are in existence and a model may be seen at the Atwater Kent Museum. (*Map I-C2*)

Morris was a wealthy merchant and banker who had helped finance the Revolution. He owned other homes in Philadelphia including the country mansion where Washington was often entertained. (p. 35) Washington wanted to make Morris the first Secretary of the Treasury, but Morris declined in favor of Alexander Hamilton. Morris was U.S. senator from Pennsylvania in the First Congress.

THE UNUSED PRESIDENT'S HOUSE (*Map I-C2*)

During Washington's administration, the state of Pennsylvania built a large, imposing President's house on 9th Street between Chestnut and Market. The State legislature apparently hoped this might help keep the national capital at Philadelphia, despite construction of the city of Washington.

The President's house was offered to John Adams when he was inaugurated in 1797, but he declined, saying that Congress would first have to authorize acceptance.

For most of his term Adams lived in the same Robert Morris mansion on Market Street which Washington had occupied.

Pennsylvania's unused President's house was vacant until 1800 when it was purchased by the University of Pennsylvania. It housed the university until 1829 when it was torn down to make way for other university buildings.

THE GERMANTOWN MANSION (*Map III-B2*)

In 1793, a deadly epidemic of yellow fever struck Philadelphia. Many government officials and private citizens fled the city. President Washington rented this house in Germantown from Colonel Isaac Franks and lived here part of the month of November.

The President and his family again rented this house in the summer of 1794.

The house became the property of Samuel B. Morris in 1834, and was eventually given by his family to the Federal Government. The oldest American "White House" still standing, it is furnished in the style of Washington's era and is open to the public.

DOLLEY MADISON'S HOUSE (*Map I-D2*)

This residence at the northeast corner of 4th and Walnut Streets, built in 1775, was purchased in 1791 by John Todd and his wife, Dolley. Todd died in 1793, and the next year his widow married James Madison, then in Philadelphia as a member of Congress from Virginia. When Madison became the fourth President in 1809, Dolley Madison won a wide reputation as White House hostess.

The First Bank
*3rd Street,
South of Chestnut
(Map I-D2)*

The Second Bank
*Chestnut Street,
East of 5th
(Map I-D2)*

BANK OF THE UNITED STATES

As Secretary of the Treasury under Washington, Alexander Hamilton set up a central bank modeled after the Bank of England. This Bank of the United States opened in 1791 in temporary quarters in Carpenters' Hall. In 1797 it moved into a building of its own on 3rd Street which is now the oldest surviving bank building in the nation.

The bank was the subject of much political and economic controversy. Thomas Jefferson had opposed it from the beginning. When its charter expired in 1811, the government did not grant a renewal. The building was purchased in 1812 by Stephen Girard, who operated his own private bank therein until his death in 1831. (p. 96)

The need for a central bank continued, and in 1816 Congress chartered the Second Bank of the United States.

Although the federal government had moved to Washington, Philadelphia remained the financial capital, and the Second Bank was located here. This too, was housed temporarily in Carpenters'

Hall, pending completion of its own building on Chestnut Street in 1824. This structure still stands and is regarded as one of the finest examples of early United States architecture.

Andrew Jackson was President when the charter of the Second Bank came up for renewal. He vetoed it and withdrew government deposits. The bank passed out of existence in 1836. A state-chartered bank was located here for a time, after which the building served as the Philadelphia Custom House for some ninety years.

(*Map I-C3*)

THE ATHENAEUM

Philadelphia also continued as the cultural capital of early America after the government moved to Washington. One reminder is the Athenaeum, a literary society founded in 1814 and still occupying a red sandstone building, in the style of an Italian Renaissance palace, on Washington Square.

A group of "young gentlemen" established the Athenaeum as "a convenient place of common resort in which leisure hours could be passed." Their reading rooms and library were located for more than twenty-five years in Philosophical Hall. (p. 48) In 1847 the Athenaeum moved into the present building which it has occupied ever since. At the rear of the second floor the lovely and spacious reading room overlooks a walled garden. Many century-old furnishings are retained.

HISTORIC COUNTRY HOUSES

The Highlands

While Philadelphia was the nation's capital, some fine country homes were built to house and entertain leaders of the young nation.

One such mansion is the Highlands, a handsome, stone Georgian house in Whitemarsh Valley, built in 1796 by Anthony Morris who was prominent in the society of the Washington and Adams administrations. In recent years, the Highlands, with its beautiful gardens, has been restored and is occupied as a private residence.

Not far away in Whitemarsh Valley (*Map II-C2*) are other celebrated houses of Philadelphia's past. One is Hope Lodge named for members of the Hope banking family of London, who purchased it in 1784. Another is Sandy Run, the Emlen family home, built about 1720. It was one of the

Andalusia

houses Washington used as headquarters before Valley Forge. A third historic house is Graeme Park originally built by Sir William Keith, Lieutenant-Governor of Pennsylvania in 1721.

One of the best known country estates of Philadelphia's Federal period is Andalusia on the Delaware River. (*Map II-C2*) It is still occupied as a private residence and is not open to the public. It was built by the Craig family in 1795. Their daughter married Nicholas Biddle, Philadelphia lawyer, diplomat, and banker, who became president of the Second Bank of the United States. One of Biddle's interests was architecture and he was responsible for many of Andalusia's outstanding features, including the Grecian front facing the river. Members of the Biddle family still live here.

(Map I-A3)

(Map I-D2)

PHILADELPHIA'S NAVAL ACADEMY

This imposing marble building occupying a sizable tract of ground at 24th Street and Grays Ferry Avenue, in South Philadelphia, was the predecessor of the United States Naval Academy at Annapolis. It was built in 1830.

In the nation's early days, young midshipmen under instruction on naval receiving ships in Boston, New York, and Norfolk were brought to Philadelphia to attend a naval school here. The building was also used as an "asylum" for retired and disabled men of the Navy and Marine Corps. As the midshipmen's school expanded, it required a separate location and in 1845 it was transferred to Annapolis. This building in Philadelphia still serves as the United States Naval Home.

MERCHANTS EXCHANGE

This is an old engraving of the Philadelphia (Merchants) Exchange as it was in 1834, and as it will soon appear again after restoration.

One of the architectural gems of the old city, this building was designed by William Strickland, the same architect who did the Naval Home and the Second Bank of the United States. In the old drawing may be seen, at the right of the Exchange, the banking house which by that time had become "Girard's Bank." At the right stands a police watch box.

95

CITY OF STEPHEN GIRARD

In June, 1776, the day before Richard Henry Lee offered his resolution for independence in the Continental Congress, a twenty-six-year-old French ship captain named Stephen Girard brought his vessel into Philadelphia to escape British warships. The high seas had become too risky for a profit-minded Frenchman, and Girard had decided to settle down on shore until the trouble blew over.

Girard made Philadelphia his home for the rest of his life. When he died at the age of eighty-one, he was one of the wealthiest men in America, and the greatest benefactor the city has ever had. In modern Philadelphia, the name Girard is commemorated everywhere. A bank, a public school, an important street, and enough business establishments to fill most of a page in the telephone book are all named Girard.

The bulk of Stephen Girard's estate is still held in trust and now amounts to about $73,000,000. It supports Girard College (*Map III-B3*), a school for the care of poor, white, male orphans between the ages of six and eighteen.

Despite his wealth, Girard's personal life was unhappy. He was blind in one eye from childhood; his young wife went insane; their only child died in infancy. Girard devoted himself to hard work and to service of his community. During the yellow fever outbreak of 1793, while many wealthy people left the city, Girard personally nursed patients in one of the municipal hospitals.

When the first Bank of the United States passed out of existence in 1811, Girard, who had been a substantial stockholder, acquired the building and established his own private bank there. During the War of 1812, he personally helped finance the United States Government. When the Treasury was able to sell only a small part of a sixteen-million-dollar bond issue, Girard and two other men subscribed for the entire remainder.

Merchant, trader, and banker, Girard was interested in agriculture as well. Almost daily he drove to his farm south of the city. The original farmhouse still remains (*Map III-B4*) and the Girard Estate has built houses on the rest of the land. Girard also owned much other real estate in Philadelphia, and his estate continues to

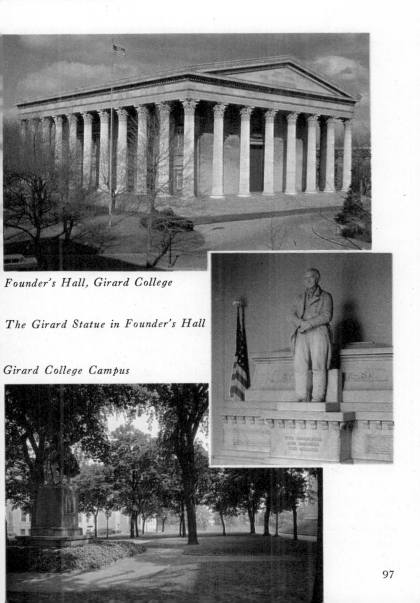

Founder's Hall, Girard College

The Girard Statue in Founder's Hall

Girard College Campus

Girard College occupies a forty-two acre farm owned by Girard when he died. The institution was formerly north of Philadelphia, but this aerial photo shows how the city has grown around it.

hold most of it, including an entire center-city block from Market to Chestnut Street between 11th and 12th Streets. (*Map I-C2*)

At his death in 1831, Girard left substantial sums of money to improve Philadelphia's waterfront and strengthen its police system. The residue of his estate was left

to establish and maintain Girard College. It has about 750 students who live at the school from the time they are admitted until graduation.

Girard's will required that a high wall be built around his school. He also provided that no clergymen should ever be admitted to the grounds, but this was not because he opposed religion. His will said:

"My desire is, that all the instructors and teachers in the college shall take pains to instil into the minds of the scholars the purest principles of morality, so that, on their entrance into active life, they may, from inclination and habit, evince benevolence towards their fellow creatures, and a love of truth, sobriety and industry, adopting at the same time such religious tenets as their matured reason may enable them to prefer."

Girard's remains are contained in a sarcophagus in Founder's Hall. His private papers, financial records, and many of his personal belongings are preserved in a memorial room in the same building.

MODERN PHILADELPHIA

City Hall Tower *overlooks Center City and Benjamin Franklin Parkway.* (*Map I-B2*)

With all its historical background, Philadelphia is also a great modern metropolis. It is a city of vastly diversified industry and commerce; it is a busy seaport; it is widely known as the city of homes; and it is a center of culture, education, and sports. The following pages illustrate for visitors some of the many aspects of modern Philadelphia.

John F. Kennedy Boulevard (*Map I-A2*)—*In the heart of the city is one of Philadelphia's most modern thoroughfares.*

Philadelphia Museum of Art (*Map I-A1*)—*A treasure house of masterpieces of all ages, and one of the leading museums of the world. The building itself is a work of art.*

The Skyline — *A view of downtown Philadelphia from the terrace of the Art Museum.*

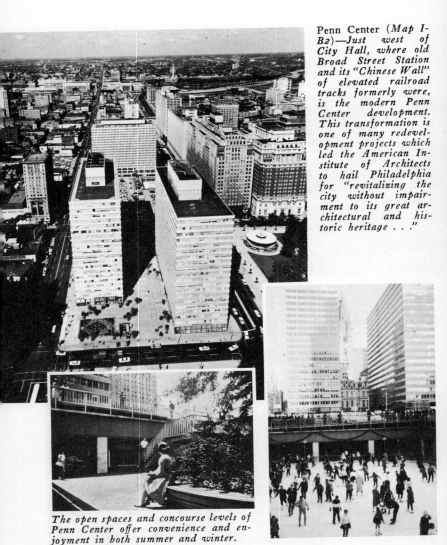

Penn Center (*Map I-B2*)—*Just west of City Hall, where old Broad Street Station and its "Chinese Wall" of elevated railroad tracks formerly were, is the modern Penn Center development. This transformation is one of many redevelopment projects which led the American Institute of Architects to hail Philadelphia for "revitalizing the city without impairment to its great architectural and historic heritage . . ."*

The open spaces and concourse levels of Penn Center offer convenience and enjoyment in both summer and winter.

The Philadelphia Orchestra—*A rare photograph of Philadelphia's renowned symphony orchestra just at the start of a concert on the stage of its own concert hall, the Academy of Music. (Map I-B3) The Philadelphia orchestra travels widely, but regularly gives eighty to ninety concerts a year in Philadelphia.*

The New Year's Parade—*An outstanding attraction for visitors to Philadelphia is the traditional parade of the Mummers or New Year's Shooters. Hundreds of thousands of spectators see this great show as it covers a long route along Broad Street and around City Hall.*

Broad Street and City Hall — *The headquarters of Philadelphia's municipal government is in the huge City Hall in Penn Square at the intersection of Broad and Market Streets. (Map I-B2)*

Robin Hood Dell—*On summer evenings as many as 30,000 persons gather here in Fairmount Park for symphony concerts under the stars. (Map IV-B2)*

Free Library of Philadelphia—*The main building of the city's extensive library system. It faces beautiful Logan Circle and the Parkway—a scene reminiscent of the Place de la Concorde in Paris. (Map I-B1)*

Tinicum Wild Life Preserve—*Inside the city limits are 205 acres of natural marshland refuge for wildfowl and game. (Map III-A4)*

Youth Study Center—*Sculpture at the front of Philadelphia's modern Youth Study Center on the Parkway. (Map I-A1)*

MAP IV

FAIRMOUNT PARK

SCALE OF MILES

0   ¼   ½   ¾   1

Queen Lane Reservoir

Woman's Medical College

HENRY AVE.

EXTENSION

ROOSEVELT BOULEVARD

ALLEGHENY AVE.

HUNTING PARK AVE.

LEHIGH AVE.

DRIVE

Robin Hood Dell

STRAWBERRY

EXPRESSWAY

Chamounix (Hostel)

GREENLAND DRIVE

DRIVE

FORD

FAIRMOUNT PARK

To Germantown

FAIRMOUNT CREEK

WISSAHICKON DRIVE

WISSAHICKON

THE WISSAHICKON

SCHOOL HOUSE LANE

RIDGE AVE.

RIVER

Gustine Lake

City Line Bridge

Falls Bridge

SCHUYLKILL

EAST RIVER DRIVE

WEST RIVER DRIVE

PRESIDENTIAL BLVD.

CITY LINE INTERCHANGE

CITY LINE AVE.

CONSHOHOCKEN RD.

FORD RD.

Belmont Reservoir

SCHUYLKILL EXPRESSWAY

MAIN ST.

RIDGE

To Main Line

CONSHOHOCKEN

106

107

FAIRMOUNT PARK

More than one hundred years ago, farsighted Philadelphians began assembling land for what is now Fairmount Park—more than 4,000 acres along the banks of the Schuylkill and Wissahickon Creek —all owned by the city and maintained as recreation area for its people.

The park is within walking distance of many residential sections of the city. It includes a summer theater, the Zoological Garden, miles of trails for hiking and horseback riding, picnic grounds, and playing fields of all types. It is criss-crossed with scenic roads and highways which provide quick transportation from one part of the city to another.

(*Map IV*)

Convention Hall and Commercial Museum—*This huge air-conditioned Convention Hall helps make Philadelphia one of the top convention cities in the U.S. Adjoining is Commercial Museum with a permanent city planning exhibit, Philadelphia Panorama. (Map III-B3)*

Army-Navy Game—*Philadelphia has been chosen repeatedly as host city for one of the nation's great sports spectacles—the Army-Navy football game. This is played in the John F. Kennedy Stadium. (Map III-B4)*

Historical Society of Pennsylvania—*Organized in 1824, this is the repository of a priceless collection of historical manuscripts, papers, books, portraits, and personal possessions of famous Americans. In its museum are exhibited mementos of William Penn, Benjamin Franklin, George Washington, and Abraham Lincoln. (Map 1-C3)*

Admiral Dewey's Flagship <u>Olympia</u>—*of the Spanish-American War, is berthed at the foot of Race Street and is open to visitors. (Map 1-D2)*

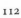

The Franklin Institute—*This handsome building on the Parkway houses the Benjamin Franklin Memorial as well as a fascinating science museum. Here is located, also, the Fels Planetarium. (Map I-A2)*

Schuylkill Expressway—*Multilevel interchange at the City Line Bridge over the Schuylkill. This highway system brings both long-distance and suburban traffic into the city.*

United States Mint (*Map I-B1*)
—*Coins have been made in Philadelphia since the birth of the country. Visitors may watch at scheduled hours. A new building for the mint is planned for Independence Mall.* (*Map I-D2*)

Police Administration Building
—*New headquarters of the Philadelphia Police Department, Franklin Square near Benjamin Franklin Bridge.* (*Map I-C2*)

Academy of Music Ballroom — *The Academy has been the center of musical activity in Philadelphia for more than a century.* (*Map I-B3*)

MUSEUMS

Pennsylvania Academy of the Fine Arts—*America's oldest art museum and art school, founded 1805 at a meeting in Independence Hall. One of the leading spirits was the artist Charles Willson Peale. In addition to the Benjamin West painting (p. 12), another famous work owned by the Academy is Peale's portrait of himself and the museum which he maintained in Independence Hall. One block north of City Hall. (Map I-B2)*

Philadelphia Museum of Art—*Contains 90,-000 works of art including 30 famous period rooms and architectural elements such as this 12th century Romanesque cloister and this Louis XVI reception room. (p. 101; Map I-A1)*

AND EXHIBITS

Academy of Natural Sciences —*America's first natural history museum founded 1812. Most celebrated of its exhibits is this dinosaur nearly two stories high. Logan Circle (Map I-B2)*

Rodin Museum (*Map I-A1*) —*An impressive collection of Rodin's work is exhibited on the Parkway in a replica of Rodin's museum in France.*

University Museum—*One of the world's leading archaeological museums is the University Museum of the University of Pennsylvania on the campus in West Philadelphia. (Map III-B3) It sponsors archaeological expeditions to many parts of the globe.*

THE PHILADELPHIA ZOO

The Philadelphia Zoological Society maintains in Fairmount Park the oldest zoo in America and one of the finest such institutions in the world, open all year and visited by about one million people annually. One of its attractions is the Children's Zoo where young people may pet ordinary farm animals. The zoo's collection of animals is unusually complete and is displayed with thoughtful imagination. Lawns, trees, and flowers make the zoo truly a zoological garden. (*Map IV-B4*)

Franklin Institute Exhibits—
*The science museum at the
Franklin Institute features exhibits which visitors may op-
erate, such as a model of a
space capsule for moon land-
ings and a full size 350-ton
steam locomotive. (Map I-A2)*

Atwater Kent Folk Museum—*This wooden, cigar-
store Indian is typical of the exhibits of Ameri-
cana and of old-time Philadelphia. The museum is
housed in the original building of the Franklin Institute erected in 1826. (Map I-C2)*

Philadelphia Maritime Museum—
*Interesting and dramatic exhibits of
the rich maritime heritage of Philadelphia and the nation. (Map I-D2)*

Aquarama—*Colorful Marine Show-
place and Theater of the Sea. Open
all year. (Map III-B4)*

American Wax Mu-
seum—*one block from
Independence Hall,
includes 200 historic,
American scenes. This
one represents Abra-
ham Lincoln writing
his immortal address
en route to Gettys-
burg, Pennsylvania.
(Map I-D2)*

THE PORT OF PHILADELPHIA

Nearly three hundred years ago, Penn chose the site of Philadelphia because it is a great natural seaport. The city is in the heart of the greatest marketing area of the nation, a hundred miles from the ocean, yet the largest seagoing vessels can berth at its piers less than a mile from City Hall.

Ship cargoes through the Port of Philadelphia lead the nation in foreign tonnage and exceed all American ports except New York in dollar value. Sightseeing boats provide interesting tours of the harbor in summer months.

Philadelphia was the birthplace of the American Navy and has always been the home of a great naval base (*Map III-B4*) where visitors at scheduled times may go aboard naval warships.

ONE-DAY TRIPS TO NEARBY PLACES

Philadelphia visitors can easily plan one-day trips to many nearby points of interest. These well-known places near the Pennsylvania-Delaware border should not be missed.

Longwood Gardens—*Only 25 miles from central Philadelphia are the renowned Longwood Gardens on the estate of the late Pierre S. du Pont near Kennett Square, Pennsylvania. This photograph shows the Fountain Garden and the Conservatory. The gardens are open to the public without charge. (Map II-A3)*

Henry Francis du Pont Winterthur Museum—*Near Wilmington, Delaware, 25 miles from Philadelphia. Contains over 100 rooms in which are displayed American domestic architecture, furniture, ceramics, metalwork, folk art, textiles, paintings, and prints of the period 1640-1840. Advance reservations required for main museum. Ten rooms in south wing open without appointment. (Map II-A3)*

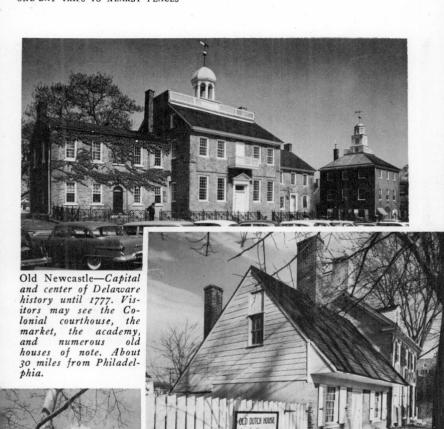

Old Newcastle—*Capital and center of Delaware history until 1777. Visitors may see the Colonial courthouse, the market, the academy, and numerous old houses of note. About 30 miles from Philadelphia.*

Old Swedes' Church—Wilmington—(*Map II-A3*)—*Built in 1698 near the site of Fort Christina, where the Swedes made their first permanent settlement along the Delaware. Old pews and original brick pavement are still to be seen.*

123

THE COUNTRY—

THE SEASHORE—

THE MOUNTAINS

Philadelphians are fortunate to have country, seashore, and mountains all near enough for a day's visit: the lush and prosperous Pennsylvania Dutch farm country —the beaches and boardwalks of the New Jersey ocean resorts— and the beautiful laurel-covered Pocono Mountains. A drive to see any or all of these can easily be included in every family's visit to Philadelphia.

Lancaster County, Pennsylvania — fifty *miles west of Philadelphia.*

Atlantic City, New Jersey — *sixty-five miles east of Philadelphia.*

The Pocono Mountains—*one hundred miles north of Philadelphia.*

PHOTOGRAPHIC CREDITS

Many of the photographs in this book were taken by Cortlandt V. D. Hubbard for the Independence Hall Association. Other illustrations are from a variety of sources, with special mention due the following:

Page

12—"Penn's Treaty With The Indians." Courtesy of the Pennsylvania Academy of the Fine Arts

25—Restored Colonial houses. Courtesy of Philadelphia Electric Company

36—Woodford Mansion photographs. Courtesy of Martin P. Snyder, Esq., Trustee, Naomi Wood Collection

37, 40, 41—Large photographs of interiors of Park Houses by Alfred J. Wyatt for *Antiques* magazine, reproduced with permission

45—Title page of *Poor Richard's Almanack* for 1733. Courtesy of The Rosenbach Foundation and the editors of The Papers of Benjamin Franklin, Yale University Press

53—Night watchman's box. Courtesy of *Life* magazine, copyright Time Inc., 1959

69—"Washington Crossing The Delaware." Photograph by Georgia A. Yeager and Robert J. Kay, reproduced with permission of the Metropolitan Museum of Art, New York

73—Painting of Chew House during Battle of Germantown. Courtesy of Mr. Samuel Chew

74—Fort Mifflin photographs. Courtesy of Mr. G. Edwin Brumbaugh

Page

76—Valley Forge chapel window. Courtesy of Alfred P. Bramnick, of the D'Ascenzo Studios, Philadelphia

78—Meschianza illustrations. From Manuel Kean Archives

80—Painting of presentation of flags to Congress. Courtesy of Continental Distilling Corporation

101, 104, 112—Photographs of downtown skyline, Robin Hood Dell and Expressway interchange. Courtesy of Philadelphia Electric Company

102, 108, 115, 120—Photographs of Penn Center in winter, rowing on the Schuylkill, Rodin's "The Thinker" and waterfront view of Delaware River. All by Howard M. Ambler

103, 113—Photographs of Philadelphia Orchestra and Academy of Music by Adrian Siegel, official photographer

113—Police Administration Building. Courtesy of Redevelopment Authority of the City of Philadelphia

121—View of naval base. Official U.S. Navy photographs

124—Lancaster County photographs by James Hess, Pennsylvania Dutch Tourist Bureau

INDEX

INDEX